AF095735

IT'S TIME TO EAT PINEAPPLE PIZZA

It's Time to Eat PINEAPPLE PIZZA

Walter the Educator

Silent King Books
A WhichHead Entertainment Imprint

Copyright © 2025 by Walter the Educator

All rights reserved. No part of this book may be reproduced in any manner whatsoever without written per- mission except in the case of brief quotations embodied in critical articles and reviews.

First Printing, 2024

Disclaimer

This book is a literary work; the story is not about specific persons, locations, situations, and/or circumstances unless mentioned in a historical context. Any resemblance to real persons, locations, situations, and/or circumstances is coincidental. This book is for entertainment and informational purposes only. The author and publisher offer this information without warranties expressed or implied. No matter the grounds, neither the author nor the publisher will be accountable for any losses, injuries, or other damages caused by the reader's use of this book. The use of this book acknowledges an understanding and acceptance of this disclaimer.

It's Time to Eat PINEAPPLE PIZZA is a collectible early learning book by Walter the Educator suitable for all ages belonging to Walter the Educator's Time to Eat Book Series. Collect more books at WaltertheEducator.com

USE THE EXTRA SPACE TO TAKE NOTES AND DOCUMENT YOUR MEMORIES

PINEAPPLE PIZZA

It's dinnertime, oh, what a treat!

It's Time to Eat
Pineapple Pizza

A yummy meal that's fun to eat.

A crispy crust, so warm and round,

With tasty toppings all around!

Cheese that melts and stretches high,

Golden brown and baked just right.

And on the top, what do I see?

Sweet pineapples, just for me!

Juicy bites of yellow gold,

A fruity taste so bright and bold.

Mixed with sauce and melted cheese,

It's pizza magic, yes, oh please!

Some say "No!" and some say "Yes!"

But I just love this yumminess!

A little sweet, a little bold,

A bite of warm and cool, behold!

It's Time to Eat
Pineapple Pizza

Grab a slice, don't let it drop,

Be careful now, it's fresh and hot!

Take a bite and chew it slow,

That pineapple zing begins to show!

One slice gone, but I want more,

Reaching for another four!

Crunchy crust and toppings tall,

I think I want to eat it all!

Mom and Dad take bites so neat,

We all agree, it's fun to eat!

Cheese and fruit in one big bite,

Pineapple pizza feels so right!

Some like peppers, some like ham,

Some say "No," but I say "Yam!"

Sweet and salty, warm and fun,

It's Time to Eat
Pineapple Pizza

Pineapple pizza's number one!

Now the tray is almost bare,

Just one slice left, we'll have to share!

Let's split it up and smile wide,

Pizza love we cannot hide!

So when you hear, "It's pizza night!"

Come to the table, take a bite!

A little sweet, a little zing,

It's Time to Eat
Pineapple Pizza

Pineapple pizza's just the thing!

ABOUT THE CREATOR

Walter the Educator is one of the pseudonyms for Walter Anderson. Formally educated in Chemistry, Business, and Education, he is an educator, an author, a diverse entrepreneur, and he is the son of a disabled war veteran. "Walter the Educator" shares his time between educating and creating. He holds interests and owns several creative projects that entertain, enlighten, enhance, and educate, hoping to inspire and motivate you. Follow, find new works, and stay up to date with Walter the Educator™ at WaltertheEducator.com

www.ingramcontent.com/pod-product-compliance
Lightning Source LLC
LaVergne TN
LVHW052014060526
838201LV00059B/4023